# JUSTICE

*Through the ages and across the world, people have always yearned for justice. And yet justice— for Earth and all its inhabitants— continues to elude us.*

Chair,
National Board
of Directors

**Connie L. Lindsey**

Chief
Executive
Officer

**Kathy Cloninger**

Vice
President,
Program

**Eileen Doyle**

Girl Scouts®

**Photographs**

**Page 19**: courtesy of www.chej.org;
**Page 32**: Photo/Rendering courtesy
of the City of New York; **Page 34**:
Los Angeles Times Photo by Gail Fisher;
**Page 36**: courtesy of Darren Schilling/
Idyllwild Arts Foundation; **Page 53**:
courtesy of Giselle Barry; **Page 83**:
© World Lung Foundation 2006; **Page 88**:
by Cynthia Koenig; **Pages 89, 91**:
courtesy of Vestergaard Frandsen;
**Page 92**: courtesy of Lung Health Image
Library; **Page 98**: Max Ortiz/The Detroit
News; **Page 100**: © 2008, California
State Parks

**Page 17**: Quote from Afton Case Study,
courtesy of the Exchange Project, www.
ExchangeProject.unc.edu

WRITTEN BY David Bjerklie

CONTRIBUTORS: Valerie Takahama, María Caban,
Rochana Rapkins, Judy Gerstel, Kathleen Sweeney

ILLUSTRATED BY Rakefet Kenaan

DESIGNED BY Alexander Isley Inc.

EXECUTIVE EDITOR, JOURNEYS: Laura Tuchman

MANAGER, OPERATIONS: Sharon Kaplan

MANAGER, PROGRAM DESIGN: Sarah Micklem

© 2009 by Girl Scouts of the USA

First published in 2009 by Girl Scouts of the USA
420 Fifth Avenue, New York, NY 10018-2798
www.girlscouts.org

ISBN: 978-0-88441-736-1

Printed in Italy

2 3 4 5 6 7 8 9/17 16 15 14 13 12 11 10 09

Text printed on Fedrigoni Cento
40 percent de-inked, post-consumer
fibers and 60 percent secondary
recycled fibers.

Covers printed on Prisma artboard
FSC Certified mixed sources.

# JUSTICE

abc

a

# Hearts + Minds

## The Start of an Equation for Justice

In 2006, a ship sailed from Europe to the Ivory Coast, in West Africa, and unloaded 400 tons of liquid that had been used to clean oil drums. The waste landed at more than a dozen public sites around the city of Abidjan. Tens of thousands of people were poisoned; 17 died.

It's illegal for a country to dump toxic waste in another country. But it still happens. That's not justice, is it?

Around the world, garbage, hazardous waste, and toxic chemicals create injustices. And those injustices are linked to the poverty, hunger, and disease endured by millions. As the green movement gains momentum, it is clear that environmental issues cannot be addressed without also addressing issues of justice. Saving the planet must go hand in hand with protecting basic rights.

# Justice.

## That's your call to action on this journey—and maybe throughout your life.

Artist, entrepreneur, inventor, corporate executive, public official, scientist—no matter what role you choose, you will have opportunities to strive for justice.

So how do you define justice? And how does your definition shape who you are and how you feel about what happens on Earth?

Once you define justice, you can strive for it—and inspire others to strive for it, too.

Many hearts and many minds working together—that's what it takes to create justice. Those hearts and minds can come together in many ways. This journey is one of them.

## *Start here, start now.*

## Profiles in Justice

As you journey for justice, you will meet women using their talents and pursuing their passions in careers that promote justice throughout the world. They are a diverse and fascinating bunch. And that makes sense, because environmental justice covers so many aspects of life. Let these women inspire you to find ways to make a difference with your unique interests and gifts. You may end up thinking about education and career possibilities that have never occurred to you before. Turn the page for a first profile to get you started.

## TAKE A NATURE BREAK!

At the heart of this journey is the belief that people everywhere should be able to enjoy the natural world and find health and strength in it. So take time to explore and enjoy the environment right outside your door, your school, your neighborhood, and your town. The journey's Nature Breaks give you new ways to strengthen your connection to the environment—and to have fun with your friends.

# Engineering: Serving Humanity with Creativity and Imagination

## Karen Panetta

dreams of seeing Engineer Barbie on toy shelves. Then she laughs and adds, "But no glasses or lab coat!" The reason, says Panetta, the worldwide director of Women in Engineering for the IEEE, the world's leading professional association for engineers, is that engineering has a bad rap.

Less than 17 percent of college engineering majors are female. "Part of the problem is that they don't see engineering as a way to serve humanity," Panetta says. "Girls think engineering is narrow and boring and that you sit in cubicles all day solving math problems and staring at a computer. But to be a great engineer, you need imagination, you need creativity, and you need to be well-rounded."

To change the stereotype, Panetta founded Nerd Girls, a network of female engineering students who show girls that it's cool to be an engineer. The Nerd Girls have designed and installed a renewable energy system to power twin lighthouses on Thacher Island, off the coast of Rockport, Massachusetts. Getting fuel and other resources to coastal islands is difficult and expensive, says Panetta. Islands need practical, low-cost, efficient power. "The U.S. Coast Guard is now adopting our design for other lighthouses. A bunch of teenage girls are now driving the way lighthouses are powered!"

Nerd Girls were also the first all-female solar car racing team in the World Solar Challenge. The project is fun and a great challenge, says Panetta, and it lets girls explore how solar power can be used for transportation.

Nerd Girl power, says Panetta, "makes a connection to a project that serves a greater purpose so that girls can see how their contribution really makes a difference."

SCALE  1½"= 1 Ft.
DRAWN BY:-
TRACED BY:-
CHECKED BY:-

SKETCH SHEET.

DATE

# BUILDING A WORLD OF ENVIRONMENTAL CITIZENS

Environmental studies combines science, technology, geography, law, labor, politics, policy, history, human relations, philosophy, ethics, and popular culture. Close to 400 colleges and universities offer degrees in environmental studies, and many have full programs devoted to justice.

Even students who major in other fields find that a course in environmental studies is an eye-opening look at the world and their place in it. They also find that environmental justice is a starting point for nearly endless possibilities. Bankers, lawyers, and doctors can use their careers to support environmental justice. Opportunities in architecture, art, design, and environmental news are also on the rise. There is mounting demand for the communication skills of writing, video, film, and webcasting.

As a result, environmental studies majors find jobs with conservation groups and research institutions, companies and consulting organizations, government agencies with municipal planning departments, and state, national, and international environmental protection commissions.

Also on the rise are training programs for green-collar jobs, which help the environment and lift low-income workers out of poverty. That's certainly justice.

But perhaps the best thing that an education in environmental justice can do is encourage the awareness that we are all environmental citizens. We all play integral roles in a larger ecosystem, and our future depends on how we meet the responsibilities of that citizenship.

# Toward the Sage Award

As you search for justice, you will have the opportunity to earn the Sage Award, and it's a fitting name for all that you will accomplish. The word sage comes from the Latin word *sapere*, to be wise. A sage is able to make wise decisions and take sensible action based on personal knowledge and experience. That means anyone can strive to be a sage. In fact, the scientific name for human beings is *Homo sapiens* and *sapiens* comes from the Latin word—you guessed it—*sapere*, to be wise.

Sage is also an herb. It belongs to the botanical genus *Salvia*, from the Latin word *salvare*, meaning to heal or to save. Sage has a long history of being used to cure everything from snakebite to memory loss. The ancient Greeks and Romans used it, as did cultures in the Middle East, India, and China. Arab physicians believed sage would increase longevity. The French call sage *toute-bonne*, meaning all is well. Recent scientific research suggests that compounds in sage may indeed boost memory.

Many cultures use sage as a fragrant herb in their cuisines. Maybe you've had pasta in sage-and-butter sauce. Or maybe your family puts sage in its Thanksgiving stuffing. More than 500 species of sage are grown throughout the world. That's a good reminder that sages, both wise people and healers, come in all varieties.

$$\begin{aligned}
&\text{Right} \\
&- \text{wrong} \\
&+ \text{courage} \\
&+ \text{compassion} \\
&+ \text{compromise} \\
&+ \text{wisdom}^2 \\
&+ \textit{your passion} \\
\hline
&\textbf{JUSTICE}
\end{aligned}$$

# Add It Up
## Your Equation for Justice

To earn the Sage Award, you will create a definition of environmental justice and an equation for achieving it. Think of it as your *equation for justice*. It must be powerful enough and comprehensive enough to share with a diverse group of people that might include leaders from community organizations, city government, and business, as well as experts from environmental groups, colleges, and medical institutions.

Your equation will include what environmental justice means to you and what it will take to bring it about.

You might be thinking: An equation? Math? What's that got to do with justice? To achieve justice many elements must come together to create a whole—just like an equation, where this plus that equals something bigger and, hopefully, better.

Your equation must invite people to think big and take a bird's-eye view of justice. At the same time, it must inspire them—and convince them to make a daily commitment to justice.

This book will step you through the journey of creating your definition, on your own, or with a group of Ambassadors. You'll take six steps to develop your equation and earn the Sage Award:

**1** LOOK HIGH, LOOK WIDE

**2** DO the MATH

**3** Be HAWK-EYED

**4** Take the SCIENTIFIC View

**5** DECIPHERING Decisions

**6** Create Your Equation & PRESENT It

Along the way, you'll find a lot of tips for how to best accomplish these steps. Just follow the Sage Award icon throughout this book. Opportunities to Nest, Soar, and Puzzle Out justice issues are optional. You'll find they help to round out your equation! You can do them with your sister Ambassadors, too. Use the tips at the back of this book to get your group organized.

As your journey unfolds, you will explore, and engage in, many issues of environmental justice. Don't feel you have to stick to just one issue throughout your journey. The more issues you explore, the more angles you will see, and, ultimately, that will help you better define environmental justice. So dive in and mix and match in any way that helps your equation for justice! And when it comes time to create and present your equation, incorporate whatever creative techniques and media you think will best capture your ideas and get people committed.

# The Journey's Sage Benefits

**As you journey toward justice, you will:**

✿ **Widen your network.** Keep track of everyone you meet and how they helped you. Invite them when you present your definition of justice. They might also become resources for college and career planning.

✿ **Gain confidence.** That helps you with, well, everything!—even any "public speaking" assignments that come your way.

✿ **Improve your ability to make wise and ethical decisions**—the kind you want the world to make. And you'll have a chance to inspire others to make them, too.

*Birds that fly in flocks will often change course, but they get to where they are going by working together.*

## Want to Be an Advocate?

Along this journey, you may find an issue you feel so passionate about that you want to become its advocate. Do! Your vision of justice can be a terrific way to launch an even larger campaign for change. A great resource on how to harness the power of advocacy is *Your Voice, Your World*. If you've already taken that Girl Scout leadership journey, you might find that some of those techniques come in handy. If you're new to the world of advocacy, just follow the steps in *Your Voice, Your World*.

# A Movement Emerges

## Have you ever poured something down the drain,

tossed something in the trash, or gotten rid of something in a way that you shouldn't have? A lot of people have. It's a bad idea, even on a small scale. But imagine that bad idea on a much larger scale.

In 1978, a company in North Carolina needed to get rid of 30,000 gallons of oil contaminated with the toxic chemical PCB (polychlorinated biphenyl). PCBs are no longer manufactured in the United States, but they were once used in all sorts of industrial applications, including as lubricants, pesticides, adhesives, coolants, and sealants. The oil was supposed to go to a facility to be reprocessed. Instead, it was sprayed along 200 miles of country roads and highways. More than 60,000 tons of contaminated soil had to be removed from those roadsides, and state officials had to decide how to dispose of it. They decided to bury the soil in Warren County, North Carolina.

When the community, which was mostly black, learned of the plan, it quickly organized a protest, which drew civil rights activists from all over the country. The protesters couldn't stop the dumping, but they made an impact. Their protest raised awareness of how environmental hazards can be linked to patterns of discrimination. Protests over other landfills followed. Community meetings and public conferences were held. Advocacy groups were formed and centers were established dedicated to the ideals of environmental justice.

A government report found that the situation in Warren County was not unusual: 75 percent of commercial hazardous-waste landfills in the South were in predominantly black communities, even though blacks made up only 20 percent of the region's population.

By 1987, a report called "Toxic Wastes and Race" was released. And in 1990, the Congressional Black Caucus and a coalition of researchers and political activists met with the Environmental Protection Agency (EPA) to discuss their concerns about discrimination and environmental hazards. The EPA studied the allegations and then created the Office of Environmental Justice. It also created this definition of environmental justice:

*"Environmental justice is the fair treatment and meaningful involvement of all people regardless of race, color, national origin, culture, education, or income with respect to the development, implementation, and enforcement of environmental laws, regulations, and policies."*

Soar

What in the EPA's definition of environmental justice speaks to your own ideas of justice? Which parts might you consider including in your equation for environmental justice?

"People . . . came and really pushed the state to live up to their word."
—Warren County community member

# CASE STUDY NO. 1
## *Love Canal*

In 1978, a neighborhood in Niagara Falls, New York, became a household name.

The story began in the 1950s, when on the outskirts of the city, an abandoned river canal, called Love Canal, was filled with 20,000 tons of chemical waste, municipal garbage, and waste from the U.S. Army. The city was growing and needed room to expand. The company that owned Love Canal sold the land to the Board of Education for $1.

© Bettmann/CORBIS

The 99th Street School was built on top of Love Canal and opened its doors to students in 1955. The neighborhood grew to include about 800 homes and 250 apartments. Very quickly, however, people started to complain about bad smells and strange substances oozing up in their yards and on the school playground.

By 1978, the state department of health found high levels of PCBs in the area. They also found an alarming increase in miscarriages, birth defects, and other medical problems. The state tried to contain the waste by building a drainage system, but eventually more than 800 families were moved out of the neighborhood.

# Lois Gibbs was

the mother of two young children, including a son in kindergarten at the 99th Street School.

While Love Canal scared people all across the nation, it made Gibbs into the country's first environmental-justice heroine. With other concerned neighbors and parents, Gibbs formed a community group to deal with the toxic threats to the neighborhood. Her efforts led to the 1980 creation of the EPA's Superfund, a program that locates and cleans up toxic waste sites throughout the country. Today Gibbs heads an organization she founded in 1981, the Center for Health, Environment and Justice, which has provided resources, assistance, and training to more than 8,000 community groups.

You may never have thought about an environmental justice issue in your hometown. But is there one? Or was there one? Scorecard.org can give you the scoop on potential hazards in your town or neighborhood. Just type in your ZIP code and see how your county stacks up in terms of polluters, chemicals released, and industrial facilities. Is lead poisoning common in your county? Do you have a Superfund site in your backyard? Search around. What do you find?

# Important Dates in Environmental History

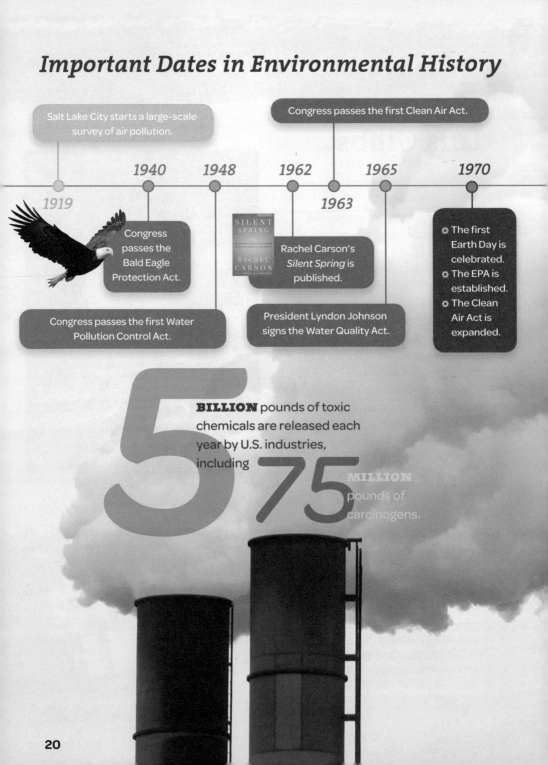

Salt Lake City starts a large-scale survey of air pollution.

Congress passes the first Clean Air Act.

**1940**    **1948**    **1962**    **1965**    **1970**

*1919*

**1963**

Congress passes the Bald Eagle Protection Act.

SILENT SPRING

RACHEL CARSON

Rachel Carson's *Silent Spring* is published.

☼ The first Earth Day is celebrated.
☼ The EPA is established.
☼ The Clean Air Act is expanded.

Congress passes the first Water Pollution Control Act.

President Lyndon Johnson signs the Water Quality Act.

**5**

**BILLION** pounds of toxic chemicals are released each year by U.S. industries, including

**75**

**MILLION** pounds of carcinogens.

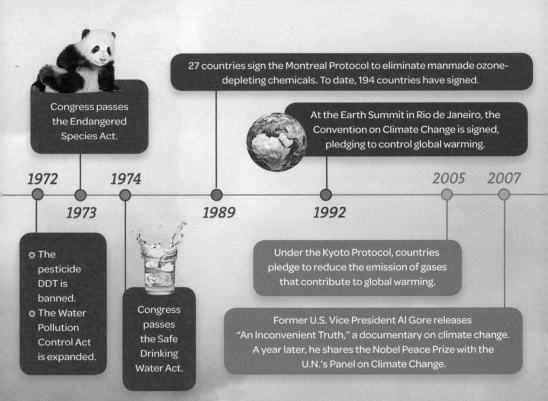

Congress passes the Endangered Species Act.

27 countries sign the Montreal Protocol to eliminate manmade ozone-depleting chemicals. To date, 194 countries have signed.

At the Earth Summit in Rio de Janeiro, the Convention on Climate Change is signed, pledging to control global warming.

**1972**    **1974**             **2005**   **2007**

**1973**        **1989**       **1992**

- ☼ The pesticide DDT is banned.
- ☼ The Water Pollution Control Act is expanded.

Congress passes the Safe Drinking Water Act.

Under the Kyoto Protocol, countries pledge to reduce the emission of gases that contribute to global warming.

Former U.S. Vice President Al Gore releases "An Inconvenient Truth," a documentary on climate change. A year later, he shares the Nobel Peace Prize with the U.N.'s Panel on Climate Change.

# ANCIENT ROOTS, TIMELESS IDEALS

You probably already have an image of justice in your mind's eye. She holds a set of scales in one hand, a sword in the other, and is usually blindfolded. This image of justice has been stamped into coins, sculpted into bronze and marble statues, and carved into facades of buildings all over the world. Its symbols capture some of our ideals of justice: scales to weigh the merits of cases and circumstances, the powerful sword of reason to determine truth, the blindfold of fairness and impartiality.

Most modern images of justice come from the Roman goddess Justitia, from whom we also get the word justice. Even among cultures that did not celebrate a goddess of justice, there have been countless myths, legends, and symbols that have served to help societies explore ideas and principles of justice.

# Soar

Dig a little and read some early myths and legends from around the world that center on justice. What do you learn from these early stories? How can these tales inform your equation for justice?

# NATURE BREAK

Find out about the camp properties that your Girl Scout Council has available for your use. Plan a day or overnight outing with your sister Ambassadors. Enjoy yourselves! You might even share some justice stories around the campfire!

# 1

# Look High, Look Wide

## As you start thinking about your equation for justice, here is your first challenge:

Look at issues from every angle and every perspective. If you can't see the whole—if you can't achieve a bird's-eye view—you run the risk of creating an injustice!

Consider this: A survey found that 80 percent of people in the United States say they are concerned about the environment. But being "concerned" means different things to different people. Some people are most concerned about pesticides in the food supply, toxic waste, or urban air quality. For others, the main concerns are disappearing rain forests, endangered species, or the depletion of atmospheric ozone.

And, of course, those concerns don't necessarily translate into action. We might all be concerned about the plight of polar bears, but are we doing anything as individuals to protect them? Thinking about them is nice and may even be heartfelt. But when it comes to environmental justice, mere thoughts aren't enough.

What we value, and what we act on, are shaped by our personal experience and our culture. Ancient cultures believed nature was sacred because humans depended on it for their lives. That dependence is why we still speak of Mother Earth or Mother Nature.

Our environmental priorities today are a mix of personal and societal. That can be a source of conflict. Understanding that different people have different priorities is the key to understanding how environmental injustices develop. It is also the key to the decision-making that can resolve them.

# Sitting at Every Stone

# Annie Petsonk is used to

working with people from all over the globe on climate issues. "It's a pretty rainbow-colored team," says Petsonk, who is International Counsel for the Environmental Defense Fund. "It's a rainbow also in terms of the disciplines that we bring together"—science, policy-making, and economics.

While lawyers usually represent the interests of one client at a time, Petsonk weighs the interests and concerns of 200 countries, all of them with a stake in climate change. Petsonk prepares her case by trying to understand the nature of global warming as well as the goals and priorities of the countries involved. The research is important, says Petsonk, because there is no simple, quick fix. "The problem is going to be with us for a long time. Everybody is going to have a chance to be part of the solution."

The importance of seeing many perspectives was a lesson that Petsonk learned in a very memorable way when she was in college. "We had a biology class, and the night before our first exam—it was Halloween night, I'll never forget it, there was a big full moon—our professor said, 'Anybody who doesn't want to study most of the night before

the first exam can come over to my house. I have a yurt in my backyard and you can meet a Cheyenne Indian medicine man named Hayemops Storm.' I was very interested! There were about twenty-five of us and we sat around in this yurt. There was this medicine man and we sat there around this fire and he didn't say anything. We didn't say anything, we just sat there. Finally, he said, 'I can see how nervous you are, you're fidgeting, you're waiting for me to say something.' Then he said, 'In my culture, you don't say anything until you've sat at every stone in the ring around the fire. So you see a problem from all the different perspectives.'"

That powerful message, says Petsonk, really stuck with her. "When I decided to go to law school, I knew I wanted to use the law to find solutions that took into account the many different perspectives of people." As she argues her case against global warming, "I try to sit at as many stones in the circle as I can."

# Soar

Think of a time when you changed your mind about something in a big way. What brought about the change? Was it more information or a new perspective? Or was it simply more time to reason out your decision? What helps you to understand a problem from someone else's perspective?

# Nest

Find five inspirational quotes, poems, or song lyrics that ignite your vision for justice. Jot them down here and visit them whenever you need a boost. Trade with your sister Ambassadors, too. Maybe you can use them in some way when you present your equation for justice.

# WASTE: YOURS, MINE, OURS

The United States generates mountains of waste and has thousands of landfills, incinerators, and storage sites where this waste is stored, recycled, or burned. But finding a place for a waste site, or a power plant or factory, is one of the toughest decisions that communities face. No one wants one in her backyard!

*Lulu*

The controversy usually begins with a **LULU, a Locally Undesirable Land Use**. Lots of folks respond to a proposed LULU with shouts of **NIMBY (Not in My Backyard)!**

*Nimby*

*Piity*

At the same time, communities may also protest, **PIITY (Put It in Their Yard)!**

Politicians who want to avoid controversy might think **NIMTOO (Not in My Term of Office)**.

*Nimtoo*

*Nimey*

Or maybe they will just feel **NIMEY (Not in My Election Year)**.

As possible locations for the LULU are narrowed down, communities likely to be affected might ask, WIMBY (Why in My Backyard)? The history of environmental justice has shown that underrepresented communities have a much more difficult time saying NIMBY to a LULU, while powerful communities have had an easy time saying PIITY to the same LULU.

## PUZZLER

Imagine that a city wants to build a soccer stadium or an airport or even a big new outdoor municipal swimming pool. As LULUs go, these are ones that most people wouldn't object to. Now imagine it will be built in your town or city. Take a look at a map. Pick three different possible locations. Now imagine a city council meeting in which residents, businesses, and politicians are all discussing which neighborhoods they think the project should be in—or not be in. What problems might be raised at the council meeting?

## Soar

Why is it that even when a law or policy has been agreed upon, people don't follow it? Is it really true that rules are meant to be broken? How can that be just? When did you last break a rule? Why? What did you gain? Who was affected by your action?

David McNew/Getty Images News/Getty Images

*Maquiladoras* is the Spanish term for export assembly plants or factories in Mexico that are operated by companies from the United States, Japan, and other countries. These factories receive tax incentives to locate along the 2,000-mile United States–Mexico border. In return, they create jobs for nearly a million Mexican workers.

An agreement between Mexico and the United States requires companies to transport any hazardous waste created by the factories back to the United States for disposal. But the EPA found that only a small fraction of the *maquiladoras* have returned the waste to the United States. Instead, it is dumped in the desert or into rivers, like the New River along the U.S.–Mexico border (shown here), from which most people in the area get their drinking water.

## CASE STUDY NO. 2
# *Fresh Kills*

For nearly 50 years, New York City had used the Fresh Kills landfill, in the borough of Staten Island, as its dumping grounds. Twenty barges, each carrying 650 tons of garbage, delivered their cargo daily to the landfill. The garbage eventually piled up higher than the Statue of Liberty, and Fresh Kills (kills comes from the Dutch word for stream or waterway) became the largest trash heap in human history.

And then, in the 1980s, Fresh Kills was full. So what could the city do with its 13,000 tons of daily garbage? One possibility was to build a new state-of-the-art incinerator to burn the garbage (there were already several in the city). The advantage of this solution was that burning the garbage would produce energy that could be converted into electricity.

The city decided that the best spot was the Brooklyn Navy Yard, a waterfront area that had once been a great shipbuilding yard. Nearby residents, however, believed that the incinerator would release toxic materials, such as mercury and dioxin. After a political fight that lasted for more than a decade, the plan was eventually dropped because of public opposition. New York now pays other states to accept most of its trash.

**PUZZLER**

See how one decision can be stopped in its tracks and abandoned? And then a new decision gets made that simply sends the problem elsewhere or covers it up? Where is the justice in that? When have you seen this happen in your life or your community?

*Over the next 30 years,* the Fresh Kills landfill will be sealed, covered in dirt, and landscaped. New York City's famous dump will be transformed into a sprawling public park with sports fields and playgrounds. It will also feature art installations, some of which may be created by Mierle Laderman Ukeles, who has been the New York City Department of Sanitation's artist in residence since 1977. One of Ukeles' proposed projects is Safe Visitor Passageways, which would allow visitors to see the Fresh Kills' remediation processes at work.

# ON THE RESERVATION

According to one study, more than 300 Native American reservations in the country must deal with environmental threats that range from toxic waste to landfills, incinerators, and unsustainable logging practices. Among the waste issues faced by reservations is the particularly scary one of radioactive waste.

This waste doesn't come out of a smokestack or a factory sewer pipe, and it doesn't smell. It is produced by mining and nuclear power generation, as well as by industry, national defense operations, and medical and scientific research. It can be in gas, liquid, or solid form, and its level of radioactivity can vary. The waste can remain radioactive for a few hours or several months or even hundreds of thousands of years.

Finding places to store this waste is a huge challenge. The biggest consideration for long-term storage is keeping it as far away from population centers as possible. But for many years that's meant that Native American reservations have been targeted as possible locations for these facilities. Many reservations are in very remote areas and are only sparsely settled.

A radioactive waste facility near a reservation would affect fewer people than one that is next to a city. But does that make it fair?

In 2008, the Navajo nation passed a comprehensive toxic waste law that will give the tribe new power to monitor and clean up hazardous waste on its 27,000-square-mile reservation in Arizona, New Mexico, and Utah. One of the first orders of business will be to try to hold private companies responsible for the hundreds of abandoned uranium mines that dot the region.

The uranium mines on this Navajo reservation have been abandoned, but the contamination of the water supply remains.

# Tatiana Deschenie is a

member of the Doodá Desert Rock collective. Doodá means "absolutely no!" in Diné, or native Navajo. The group opposes Desert Rock, a coal-burning power plant proposed for the Four Corners region, near Burnham, New Mexico. With two power plants already marring ancestral lands, Tatiana decided to use her painting to make a statement against the power plant. "Art can definitely push a message," she says. "It can get people to notice an issue."

Tatiana, who describes herself as five-eighths Navajo with some Hopi and Filipino ancestry, grew up in Farmington, New Mexico, a few miles from the reservation. "Native American culture is cherished in my family," she says. In 2008, at "Connections: Earth + Artist = A Tribute Art Show in Resistance to Desert Rock," Tatiana's painting "What Is Beauty?" received an Honorary Youth Entry award. She was the youngest artist in the show. Her canvas features smokestacks and color drips against a desert landscape.

"I believe we should have a very balanced relationship with the natural world. Obviously now we're in a state where that balance is very threatened," says Tatiana.

During the same summer as her award-winning art show, Tatiana attended College Horizons, a workshop for Native Americans held at Lawrence University in Appleton, Wisconsin. There she ignited a crowd of 150 with a talk about the Desert Rock power plant. "If you want to get your voice heard," she says, "you have to speak up."

# TALES FROM
# THE TRASH CAN

A midden is the name given to the pile of refuse or hole in the ground used as a mini-landfill by households or villages hundreds and even thousands of years ago. Archaeologists have long studied these ancient heaps for clues to how people lived.

A kitchen midden would often include remnants of cooking fires and scraps of food, bones, and shells, as well as broken tools, pieces of clay pots, and bathroom waste. From this humble evidence, archaeologists have been able to decipher what people ate, how healthy they were, whom they traded with, and even when times of plenty gave way to lean times and starvation.

In 1973, researchers from the University of Arizona started looking at exactly what we throw away. They discovered that what people say they eat and what their garbage cans reveal they actually eat are two different things. As one example, people claim they eat much more asparagus than they really do! Another is that the average amount of garbage we produce is increasing, even with increased recycling. The researchers found that construction debris accounted for 20–30 percent of the refuse and paper products for 40–50 percent. Twenty percent of all household waste was food-related.

The very design of modern landfills slows the process by which even biodegradable materials disappear. The Arizona team found preserved but still readable newspapers, along with 15-year-old hot dogs and an ear of corn that had survived for nearly two decades!

# WASTE NO MORE!

A growing number of environmentalists think the real challenge is not to manage waste, but to do away with it altogether. Is that possible?

In the early years of the environmental movement, the expression cradle-to-grave described what was then a very ambitious goal: Industry would have to take full responsibility for any pollution it created. And it would have to be responsible for the disposal of any waste it produced and any products it created once their useful life ended.

Now the ultimate goal is cradle-to-cradle responsibility. Industry must design products in a way that produces no waste. Instead, every component of the product would be reused as a resource or raw material for other products. There would be no waste to bury or burn—ever.

Consider the debate about paper versus plastic grocery bags or even the sturdy reusable bags made from recycled plastic. Paper bags require the logging of millions of trees, but are biodegradable. Plastic bags require millions of barrels of oil to produce and will last for thousands of years. A cradle-to-cradle solution would be a compostable bag you could just toss in your garden to help it grow.

# Soar

Imagine a product that does the environment good. What would it be?

Need a little space where you can stop and think? A little quiet time each day or week helps us be purposeful about our actions. Clear one corner of your nest from all clutter—no phone, no TV, no piles of homework or college applications. Add in any of these: a candle, a journal and pen, an inspirational poem or other reading material, soothing music.

Commit to spending 10 minutes of quiet time here a few times a week. Ask yourself this: What do I value? How do I act on (or not act on!) that value?

# Nest

# CASE STUDY NO. 3
## *Biofuels*

Just a few years ago, growing gasoline seemed like an environmental dream. But engineers have figured out how to turn crops into fuel—maybe too successfully. Biofuels are soon expected to be a $100 billion business, and that has already meant a gold rush for farmers and companies around the world. Land that was once used to grow crops for food, especially corn and soybeans, is now being used to produce ethanol and biodiesel.

The burning of biofuel releases carbon that is reabsorbed by the next year's crop of plants used to make more biofuel. But growing biofuels takes away land from growing food. And that has created rising food prices around the world, which has hurt poor people most. The amount of corn it takes to produce enough ethanol to fill the tank of an SUV would feed one person for a year.

Now a growing number of experts are questioning whether biofuels actually produce fewer greenhouse gases than coal or oil. The efficiency of a biofuel turns out to depend on several factors: the plant it is made from, the energy it takes to turn the plant into fuel, and the land the plant is grown on. Harvesting corn in Iowa for fuel instead of food doesn't change the cornfield's footprint; clearing rain forest to plant oil palms, however, creates an entirely new environmental footprint.

In Indonesia, the No. 1 reason that rain forest is cut down is to make room for plantations of oil palms used to make biodiesel. It's happening in Malaysia and other parts of Southeast Asia, too. Because of this destruction, greenhouse gas emissions are actually increasing! Deforestation now accounts for 20 percent of all carbon released into the atmosphere.

Sugarcane, one of the most efficient sources of ethanol, now supplies 45 percent of Brazil's fuel needs. But a three-way competition for land among cattle ranchers and soybean and sugarcane farmers is destroying the country's rain forest and savanna lands.

Biofuels have become big business, and many experts fear that their negative impact on food prices, deforestation, and global warming will be felt for many years. But researchers are also trying to find ways to make biofuels sustainable, by making them from agricultural waste such as cornstalks, wood chips, lawn trimmings, forest and construction debris, and even garbage. Livestock manure and used vegetable oil from restaurants are being tapped, too. And one of the most promising sources for biofuel is single-celled plants called algae that can be grown in industrial-size vats. These new sources, known as biomass, could play a crucial role in the next generation of biofuels.

## Two Ways to Turn Plants into Fuel

1. Starch and sugar are extracted from a plant with high sugar or starch content, such as corn, beets, or sugarcane. The starch and sugar are then fermented with yeast in a process identical to making wine or beer. The ethyl alcohol, or ethanol, that is produced can then be burned in engines that have been specially modified.

2. Oil is extracted from plants high in natural oils, such as soybeans or palm fruits, in a process similar to squeezing oil from olives. The oil is then transformed into fuel called biodiesel.

# Start Your Equation!

By now, you can see that a perspective that is both wide and high provides context and lets you to see the many sides of a  situation more clearly. So take a bird's-eye view of an example of environmental injustice. It can be a historical case or one in your own backyard, or one mentioned in this book that you gather some more research on.

Investigate how the injustice developed. What was the source and who was, or is, affected? Consider the context and as many sides of the story as you can. Who was at the table when a decision was made? Who was not? What impact did that have?

Your equation for justice is now beginning. How does looking at various sides of an environmental problem shape your view of the injustice? How could what you learned help resolve the injustice or avoid a future injustice?

The highest fliers of all might be bar-headed geese, which are believed to hit altitudes of nearly 30,000 feet. Heading in the other direction, emperor penguins can dive nearly 2,000 feet deep into the waters of the ocean off Antarctica. That's some perspective!

# 2

# Do the Math

## As you take in the big picture of environmental justice,

remember to focus in closely, too—by making your commitment to environmental justice a daily habit. You might be thinking: *There are 6.7 billion people in the world! What I do as an individual won't make any difference at all!*

But you have more clout than you think. When you establish goals and then achieve them, you set an example for others. And those others, in turn, can inspire still more people. If each week you convince just three people to help you make a difference and they each do the same, after four weeks you will have 121 people on board. In a month, you'll have 2,391,484 people—more than the population of Maine and Montana! That's some impressive math! Your inspiring example can harness the power of many!

The Do the Math items throughout this chapter offer ways to set change in motion right away and inspire others to join you. Pick two to stick with, on your own or as a team. Do the Math is Step 2 toward the Sage Award. But your commitment to Do the Math will be ongoing. After all, math is essential to any equation!

## Do the MATH

### HOW'S YOUR GARBAGE?

Each person in the U.S. produces about 4.4 pounds of garbage a day. If everyone in your school could cut their garbage in half for one year through composting, recycling, and reducing unnecessary packaging, how much less trash would have to be trucked to a landfill? To help you visualize the impact you could make, use an adult elephant as your unit of weight measure. Or make it a rhino or a sumo wrestler. Do the calculations. How many elephants (or whatever!) of trash could your school save from the dump? What if your whole town or city did the same? Now that's a herd of difference!

### COUNT YOUR TRASH!

Get a pair of rubber gloves and conduct your own garbology research. Sort the waste into categories, such as food, wrappers, cans, bottles, paper, and plastic. Record exactly what your family throws out for three days. If you have nerves—and a nose—of steel, try it for a full week!

Which wastes could be reduced and how? Is there packaging you could avoid, material that you could recycle, or things that you could do without? Make those reductions a daily commitment!

# OUR HUMAN FOOTPRINT

Issues of environmental justice are loaded with math. One that is particularly loaded is the carbon footprint. That's a measure of the impact we have on the environment in terms of the greenhouse gases we produce—mainly carbon dioxide, but also methane and a few others. Efforts to slow global warming today are focused on reducing our carbon footprints.

An even bigger footprint is our ecological footprint. That's the measure of our total impact on Earth's ecosystems and resources. It is the sum total of all the resources we consume and, in turn, all the wastes we produce.

Imagine your personal ecological footprint. Start with the land needed to grow the food you eat. How big a farm would be needed to grow everything you eat in a year, from chocolate banana milkshakes to pepperoni pizzas?

Then there's the water drawn from wells, lakes, and rivers that you use to drink, bathe, wash clothes every day. Would it fill a swimming pool in a year?

Building materials are also part of your footprint, as is absolutely every single thing you own or use. Your footprint includes all of the raw materials and all of the energy that it takes to manufacture those goods, as well as the energy used to light and heat your home and fuel your car or the city bus you ride.

And every single thing you throw away, every bit of garbage, every waste produced in the course of making all of the things you own and use—all that goes into your footprint as well.

## UNEQUAL FOOTPRINTS

Our footprints raise tough questions about environmental justice on a global scale. The average footprint of a person in the United States is much, much bigger than the average footprint of a person living in Africa or Asia. When it comes to energy, for example, the United States, which accounts for just 5 percent of the world's population, burns more than 25 percent of all the coal, oil, and natural gas extracted from the planet each year.

The comparison is also lopsided when it comes to food, water, garbage, and nearly everything else. The United States and Europe spend far more on cosmetics than it would cost to provide clean water and sanitation for the rest of the world. Same for ice cream, perfume, or pet food.

## How can that be fair?

When it comes to environmental footprints and justice, there are three basic, but very important facts we must face:

Date.
Nearly 3 billion people in the world live on less than $2 a day, which means they have too little food, water, energy, medicine, or housing.

Date.
The planet could not support 6.7 billion people if each one consumed resources and produced waste like an average American.

Date.
The consequences of the consumption habits of wealthy nations often directly affect the health and well-being of people in poor parts of the world.

The Worldwatch Institute calculates that if all of the biologically productive land on the planet was shared equally, each person would have a bit fewer than 2 hectares (about five football fields) to produce resources and absorb wastes.

In reality, the average American uses nearly

# 10
**HECTARES**

The average Mozambican uses less than

**.5**
**HECTARES**

## Do the
# M A
# + H

## GASOLINE'S FOOTPRINT

Calculate the carbon impact of burning 1 gallon of gasoline. To keep it simple, start at the gas station. A gallon of gasoline weighs a bit more than 6 pounds, and 85 percent of it is carbon and the rest is hydrogen. So there are 5.25 pounds of carbon in a gallon of gasoline. When gasoline burns, the carbon and hydrogen separate. The hydrogen combines with oxygen in the air to form water ($H_2O$), and the carbon also combines with oxygen to form carbon dioxide ($CO_2$). Through the miracle of chemistry, burning 6 pounds of gasoline produces 20 pounds of carbon dioxide and 15 pounds of water vapor!

**20 POUNDS $CO_2$**

**GAS** **= >** **+**

**6 POUNDS**

**15 POUNDS $H_2O$**

Now, how about the footprint of a glass of chocolate milk? First, there's the fuel used to harvest and transport the cacao beans grown on plantations in the tropics. If the land was cleared of its natural forests, that's more carbon. And then there's the energy it takes to turn the ingredients into chocolate syrup or powder, the materials for packaging, and transportation to the grocery store.

Now the milk. There's the carbon impact of growing the grain or alfalfa to feed the cow (which involves fuel for farm equipment plus fertilizer, which releases nitrous oxide, a greenhouse gas nearly 300 times more potent than carbon dioxide). While Bessie is producing milk, she is also producing gas (methane) and manure (more methane). Methane is a greenhouse gas that is 20 times more potent than carbon dioxide. There's also the carbon cost of processing and transporting the milk. If it is shipped in a plastic container, there's the carbon cost of the petroleum and energy used to make the plastic.

It may seem silly to calculate the carbon footprint of a glass of chocolate milk, but it's a good example of how easy it is to take our footprint for granted. Everything we do in life results in carbon dioxide emissions. But that shouldn't lead us to think we can't do anything about it. There is widespread agreement on reliable ways to reduce our carbon impact.

Many online tools can help you calculate the carbon impact of daily life. Start with the government Web sites from the U.S. Department of Energy and the Environmental Protection Agency, but then search around until you find one that you like. Sites like carbonrally.com turn green efforts into competitive fun. Form a team, set a carbon-reduction goal, and then challenge another team to see who can get there first!

Energy conservation measures alone could cut U.S. fossil fuel consumption by 30 percent.

Another way to think of energy efficiency is in terms of future power plants that would *not* have to be built. Adopting household-appliance efficiency standards would eliminate the need for 127 new U.S. power plants by 2020. Residential air-conditioner efficiency standards would end the need for another 43 power plants. Stronger standards for commercial air-conditioning would eliminate 50 plants. Increasing the energy efficiency of new buildings over the next 20 years would save another 170 plants. And improving the energy efficiency of existing buildings would save 210 plants. That's 600 power plants no one would ever have to live near! So find a way to increase your energy efficiency right now.

## Big Sister, Big Clock

City officials in Bangkok, Thailand, conducted an experiment one evening. They asked all major TV stations to show an image of a big dial with the city's current use of electricity displayed. Residents were asked to turn off unnecessary lights and appliances. Viewers could then watch the dial register the reduction of 735 megawatts in electrical demand, enough to shut down two coal-fired power plants.

**PUZZLER**

Catalogchoice.org and DMAChoice.org estimate that 19 billion catalogs are sent through the mail each year at a cost of 53 million trees and 5.2 million tons of $CO_2$. That's a big footprint! But take another look. Could mail-order catalogs actually save carbon? The mail-order industry claims that it saves millions of automobile miles (shopping trips) each year. What do you think?

# "1 + 1 + 1 = 6"

## Cathy Zoi,

founding CEO of the Palo Alto, California-based Alliance for Climate Protection, has an ambitious goal for the United States: a switch to 100 percent renewable electricity by 2018. The Alliance's "RePower America" and "We" campaigns call for a power grid retrofit, and a portfolio approach of wind, solar, and geothermal energy is part of the equation, but "a third of it," she says, "is about energy efficiency."

A geologist and engineer, and a passionate policymaker, Zoi often speaks of clean energy's "yes factor." "This isn't a technology problem," she says. "It isn't some sort of Jetsons-like vision that hasn't been invented yet."

Deeply impressed by a "Keep America Beautiful" public service announcement she saw as a child in the 1970s, Zoi understands the power of good messaging. In the ad, a Native American canoes through a polluted river, then turns to the camera in tears. A voice-over intones, "People start pollution. People can stop it."

For Zoi, language is crucial. "I've not used the term 'alternative energy' for years and years and years," she says. "To me, 'alternative' has a connotation of non-mainstream, and what we need to be aiming for is mainstreaming these technologies."

The We campaign often produces ads so "sticky," its membership of 2 million passes them on via e-mail and social networking sites. The result is "not 1+1+1=3," Zoi explains. "It's 1+1+1=6." This "wonky arithmetic" works exponentially, as in squared, cubed, zillioned!

"What's in fact uplifting to me about the energy crisis," Zoi adds, "is that individually we can't solve it, but together we can. The zeitgeist of 'We' is very, very important."

*Do the*

# M A
# + H

## AND GET A NATURE
## BREAK, TOO

One quarter of all car trips in the United States are shorter than a mile; more than a third are less than two miles. From 1977 to 1995, the number of walking trips taken by adults declined by 40 percent. Find ways to incorporate walking into your routine and calculate the miles not driven. If Americans spent 30 minutes walking or cycling instead of taking the car for short trips, they'd take a big bite out of greenhouse gas emissions and in the process also shed more than 3 billion pounds! And that's not all. A British study concluded that walking actually "saves" time. The researchers estimate that for every minute you walk, you add about three minutes to your lifespan.

*Keep track and see if you can add five hours to your life this week!*

# YOUR FOOD, YOUR CHOICE

Coal-burning power plants and pollution from cars are among the most commonly cited sources of greenhouse gas emissions. But experts also point to another source: our diet. The solution, says the head of the UN's Nobel Prize–winning International Panel on Climate Change, may surprise you: Eat less meat.

How can food choices hurt or help the planet? Dietary choices have a great impact on the environment. In the United States, livestock production requires huge quantities of land, water, and petroleum for the fuel, fertilizer, and pesticides needed to grow crops to feed the livestock. In fact, most corn, soybeans, and grains grown in the U.S. are either fed to animals or turned into fuel.

Is feeding staple crops to animals an efficient way to produce food? According to ecologist David Pimentel of Cornell University, nearly 800 million people could be fed with the grain currently fed to U.S. livestock. That's food for thought!

## "Green" Eggs & Ham?

Just as citizens have lobbied to reduce packaging and adopt biodegradable containers, they are also pushing for ways to have their meat while lightening the environmental footprint of livestock production. Groups like the American Grassfed Association, which was founded in 2003 and now represents 400 producers across the United States, are spreading the word on practices, such as intensive "rotational grazing," that are environmentally healthier alternatives to factory-style feedlots. Their aim is less soil erosion, less pollution, and a decrease in the use of fossil fuel. "When consumers ask for grass-fed meat, ranchers respond," says Carrie Balkcom, executive director of the AGA. "We know that animals raised entirely on pasture are better for the environment than the big concentrated animal feeding operations. Grassfed meat has a lighter environmental impact."

## Gassy Problem

Livestock production takes up nearly 30 percent of all usable land in the world. It also produces nearly 20 percent of all greenhouse gases—more than all types of transportation combined. It is the methane gas that is naturally produced by digestion in livestock and in manure that is the big problem. Each ton of methane has the same greenhouse effect as 20 tons of $CO_2$. The amount of manure the United States meat industry produces is 130 times the volume of human waste—that's about 5 tons of manure for every person!

Raising beef cattle is also a major factor in deforestation. A New Jersey–size chunk of South America's Amazon rain forest disappears each year. Between 60 and 70 percent of the destruction is caused by ranchers clearing land to create pastures for cattle. Burning forests to clear land also releases huge amounts of $CO_2$.

## PUZZLER

On average, Americans eat 220 pounds of meat per year—twice the global average. In 1950, annual meat production worldwide was 44 million tons; today it is 284 million tons. That number is expected to double by 2050. As developing nations raise their standards of living, their citizens want to eat more meat. Is it fair to tell them they shouldn't? Should Americans be held accountable for the environmental impact of their diet? A Japanese study calculated that 2.2 pounds of beef produce the $CO_2$ equivalent of driving a car 155 miles. What's your beef mileage?

## Soar

There are so many interesting food topics to think about and study as you soar into your future. Who will grow what, raise what, and eat what where? You can make a difference as an agricultural scientist or engineer, as an ecologist, botanist , or farmer. What food ideas do you have?

## Nest

Where do you get your protein? Sages (and Ambassadors!) need energy. If most of your protein comes from meat, try adding in some variety. You might try cheese, yogurt, beans (there are so many kinds!), and nuts. And did you know that most vegetables contain 10 to 15 percent protein? In fact, peas, green vegetables, and beans have more protein per calorie than meat. Plus, they're rich in nutrients.

*Romania's Lake Bicaz is filled with plastic and other garbage left behind by visitors to its once scenic shores.*

# WATER, WATER EVERYWHERE

In the 1980s, portable $H_2O$ caught on fast in fitness clubs, restaurants, grocery stores, and, eventually, vending machines all across the country. Carrying around a bottle of water in your backpack or handbag was a sign of an active, healthy lifestyle. Fashionable holsters were designed just for water bottles. Magazines even noted which brand of water celebrities favored.

Today more than 20 billion bottles of water are bought in the United States every year and water drinkers can choose from among hundreds of brands. You can choose water from 10,000-year-old glaciers, icebergs, snow-capped mountains, underground springs the world over, and even rainwater collected from the far corners of the planet.

Three-quarters of all Americans drink some bottled water and 20 percent say they drink only bottled water, which means that they could easily be spending over $1,000 a year for stuff that comes out of the tap for pennies!

**100**

The average number of **GALLONS** of water each person in the United States uses daily

**50**

The number of **GALLONS** each person uses in Europe

**8**

The number of **GALLONS** each person uses in Africa

**22 BILLION** The number of bottles of water bought in the United States in 2007

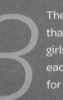

**3** The number of **HOURS** that many women and girls in rural Africa spend each day fetching water for their families

# THE BOTTLE DEBATE

But now the boom in bottled water has landed it smack in the middle of an environmental justice debate. Here's why:

Bottled water costs more per gallon than gasoline. In 2007 people in the United States spent $12 billion for the convenience of portable water. That's more than the country spent going to movies all year!

It takes 17 million barrels of oil to manufacture the plastic bottles (and that doesn't include the millions of barrels of oil burned to transport bottled water all around the country). Manufacturing the plastic bottles also consumes 3 gallons of water for each gallon of water bottled.

Less than 15 percent of all plastic water bottles are recycled. Americans toss them into the trash at the rate of 700 bottles per second. That's 60 million a day. And if you count all beverages in cans and bottles, we toss out nearly three times that number every day.

## So a simple bottle of water has a very big environmental footprint.

A growing number of groups are asking people to boycott bottled water and focus on the world's life-and-death water issues. They believe that clean water should be a basic human right.

Students in high schools and colleges around the country have been some of the most passionate protesters. Some schools have set up "bottled-water-free zones," while other are signing up fellow students to take the TOTB (think outside the bottle) pledge. One protest involved sending notes in empty water bottles to the president of a large corporation that sells bottled water. Other groups are trying to make tap water hip by promoting the use of cool and colorful reusable bottles.

Politicians are getting into the act, too. The U.S. Conference of Mayors passed a resolution that brought attention to the environmental footprint of bottled water, and a growing number of cities across the country have banned bottled water from government-sponsored events.

Bottled water companies are taking the hint. Some are responding by trying to make their footprint smaller. A few are even using some of their profits to address water issues in the developing world.

# Soar

What is your relationship to bottled water? Do you drink a lot of it, shun it, have it now and then when it's offered to you? What can you change in your daily life to reduce the use of bottled water—either your own use of it or the use you see around you?

Think about your own nest, the place you call home! What do you have—possessions, habits, or routines—that makes your life more convenient? A TV in every room? Ditto for computers or music-playing devices? Habits like buying clothes you wear only once or twice? Or the newest cell phone, even though your old one was just fine? Do you ask for a ride when you could walk or bike? What else?

What conveniences would you give up if you knew it could ultimately contribute to solving an injustice somewhere on Earth? How hard is it to give something up? Try it! While you're at it, ponder this: What are people willing to give up, in a big way, to save Earth and all her inhabitants? What stops people from pitching in?

# Nest

# One Is Better Than None

# Jennifer Languell

is an engineer who spent a year traveling to Greenland, Australia, South Africa, the Louisiana Gulf Coast, and many other places to test cutting-edge scientific theories and ideas to help the environment. One important lesson she learned transcended geographical boundaries.

"I think the biggest thing I learned is we're not trying to save the planet, we're trying to save our way of life," she says.

Take the Inuits in Greenland, who have earned their living for six generations by fishing. "Now this generation can't do that because of climate change. It's impacted their way of life," Languell says. "They're not trying to stop ice from melting. They're not trying to stop pollution. They're trying to save the fact that fishing is how they've always made a living."

Languell was one of three members of a "task force" on the Discovery Channel's "Project Earth" environmental series. Along with a physicist and an entrepreneur, she traveled the world to talk with scientists and conduct experiments based on their ideas. For example, they met with an engineer who has a plan to get energy from a turbine that harnesses the wind at 1,000 feet above sea level. Another scientist they met wants to prevent the Arctic ice shelf in Greenland from melting by covering it with blankets that reflect sunlight and block the wind.

As important as such big, bold ideas may be to stemming climate change, Languell is also in favor of ordinary people taking smaller actions to help save resources and reduce waste. That point was brought home to her one day in Greenland when she noticed someone using his fingers to clean every last scrap of food from his plate. At first she thought, "That's just so weird." Then she realized he was cleaning his plate to help save water.

"When you're carrying your water from point A to point B, and water is such a valuable resource, it's so wasteful to use excess water to simply clean a dish," Languell says.

But it doesn't have to be all or nothing, she says. "I love my shoes and I love taking long showers, but my front yard has no grass. So I save 100,000 gallons of water a year by having native vegetation and no irrigation. But I like a nice shower," she says.

"Not everyone can put compact fluorescent bulbs everywhere. So put them where you can. One is better than none!"

## Do the Math!
## Add It In!

The Girl Scout Law says it all—use resources wisely! Which Do the Math suggestions are you following through on? What does actively cutting down tell you about your equation for justice? What would it take to get more people doing the math? Add in your initial thoughts here as you keep Doing the Math!

E

Voyager 1

09

# 3

# Be Hawk-Eyed

*Continuing along the road to justice, here's your next challenge:*

## Analyze your information and your sources.

It can be very difficult to determine whether news coverage of environmental issues is thorough or even accurate. And savvy businesses are doing their best to capitalize on environmental issues. Green marketing is big business.

What exactly does "green" mean in the business world? What does "eco-friendly" or "natural" tell us about a product? When companies try to look green without really being green, environmentalists call it "greenwashing." Sometimes greenwashing is fraud. In many cases, it's simply the result of exaggerated good intentions.

# BEWARE OF GREENWASHING

To help consumers make sense of green marketing, a number of organizations have sprung up to investigate industry claims. A study by TerraChoice found that out of 1,000 randomly chosen "green" products, 99 percent were guilty of greenwashing to some degree. Some products claimed to be organic but offered no proof; some claimed to be natural but contained "natural" toxins like arsenic; some were energy-efficient but contained hazardous materials. Even car companies are guilty of greenwashing. A report by the Union of Concerned Scientists found that half of all hybrid cars are no more fuel-efficient than nonhybrid models.

The U.S. Federal Trade Commission is working to establish standards for green marketing claims. But for now, consumers must beware— and be informed.

# Eye on the Media

Unusual weather immediately prompts the question: Is this another sign of climate change? And it is almost impossible these days to pick up a magazine and not find a celebrity who is urging us to do our part to save the planet.

But there is so much news coverage of environmental problems that it is important to cultivate careful reading habits. So analyze any news stories you collect.

# Gwendolyn Hallsmith

says the best way to get involved in environmental justice is to first look at your own life. "Our culture has created superconsumers," she says. "To me, one of the most important things young adults can do is to be mindful of what they're buying—the impact on the environment, whether it's made by people being paid fair wages—and to be mindful of how everything they do either contributes to or detracts from the goals they're trying to achieve. We could change the world by changing our buying habits."

As the director of planning and community development for Montpelier, Vermont, Hallsmith is working to develop a renewable biomass energy plant that would provide buildings in the downtown area with heat and electricity powered by wood chips and pellets.

She's also passionate about issues of environmental justice. "Most people put the environment and the economy in opposite camps," she says. "But you can't achieve environmental integrity and protection without also simultaneously achieving social and economic justice." Poverty, she insists, is one of the biggest environmental problems we have.

Hallsmith is much sought after worldwide as a speaker and consultant on issues of social justice and the environment. But she also hits the streets through the Residential Energy Conservation Program, going into people's homes to show them how to conserve energy through simple changes, like using weather-stripping. And when Hallsmith is on the street, she's either walking or on her bike—which has studded snow tires for the Vermont winter!

PUZZLER

Advertising tries to convince us that we are what we buy, and people often form opinions about others according to the brands they wear. But what we buy—or don't buy—can also be a positive reflection of our values. What do your purchases say about your views on the environment? What about consumerism might you add to your equation for justice?

# Nest

Search through newspapers, magazines, and Web sites to find a few images that clearly show injustice. Now find a few that evoke the feeling of justice. If the mood strikes, go all out and make an (in)justice collage. Consider this: If we can so clearly see what is just and what is not, why is it so hard to achieve justice?

Think about how you might use these images or others when you create and present your equation for justice.

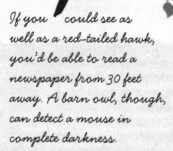

*If you could see as well as a red-tailed hawk, you'd be able to read a newspaper from 30 feet away. A barn owl, though, can detect a mouse in complete darkness.*

# Add to Your Equation!

We live with a constant deluge of information about the environment, including news stories and seemingly endless green marketing and advertising campaigns. Environmental themes are even tapped for movies and TV shows. So you must carefully evaluate the language, sources, claims, and narrative formulas used to tell environmental "stories." That calls for being hawk-eyed—or owl-eyed!

Collect 10 examples of news stories on environmental issues and 10 examples of advertising or marketing that mention the environment. Categorize the examples by environmental issue, geography, urgency, or other criteria. Try a few different sorting methods. What conclusions or generalizations can you make about the topics and the approaches of the news stories and the advertisements? How do the stories and the ads compare? How do they differ?

What environmental issues are covered most? Are these issues the most important or most urgent? What other reasons might explain which issues are covered most?

Which news stories or ads provoked your curiosity, doubt, or anger? Were there cases of injustice? Were they identified as such? Did you find examples in the ads of effective ways to capture people's attention and motivate them to act that you might use in your equation for justice?

**Take a closer look at the news stories.** Do they clearly explain the environmental issues and their risks? Do they allow you to compare the various risks being written about? Do they explain who is most affected by the environmental issue? If the stories involve decisions that have been made or need to be made, do they explain who is involved in the decision-making? How is the research behind the story presented? Do scientists agree on what is happening, what it means, and what should be done? If not, how is the uncertainty explained? Is more research required, or do the doubts and disagreements represent various opinions or concerns?

Circle any words that jump out at you. Is the tone optimistic or pessimistic? Does the choice of words make it clear how the writer feels about the issue? Is the writer warning readers or challenging them in any way? Or is the writer remaining neutral and simply presenting various sides of an issue?

Who does the writer cite as authorities? How are politicians and leaders woven into the article? Are scientists portrayed as neutral and objective or do they express their opinions? How are other people portrayed? What purpose do they serve in the story?

Do some articles seem to follow similar narrative patterns? How would you group certain stories together and why? What elements in the story speak to you most clearly or most persuasively? Why?

Parakeets, budgies, mynahs, and macaws are all talented mimics. The real trick is to take in what's around you, form your own opinion, and speak it!

# Take the Scientific View

## *Science is integral to environmental justice.*

Science isn't all clear-cut facts, though. It's often about weighing risks and benefits.

We all live with environmental risks. There might be a landfill close to our community, or a factory or power plant down the road. There might be nearby highways packed with cars, or farmland as far as the eye can see. The unavoidable fact is that no matter where we live, our environment affects the water we drink, the air we breathe, and the food we eat.

Scientists try to measure potential dangers from environmental threats through a process called risk assessment. It is a powerful tool, but it isn't perfect. It can provide us with critical information, but that doesn't mean the answers are simple.

Let's say **PESTICIDES** have been detected in a town's water supply. What is the chance that people will actually experience health problems if they drink this water? Is there a level of the pesticide in drinking water that won't pose a health risk? How much of the water would someone have to drink for it to be dangerous?

Scientists have found that risks vary according to many factors. **LEAD** can have especially serious consequences for infants and young children, whose bodies are still developing. **MERCURY** can have devastating effects on the unborn children of pregnant women. Within any community there will be people at higher risk for harm, often for reasons that are not obvious, such as genetic background. Not all environmental threats are equal and not all individuals exposed to the same threat will react in the same way.

Researchers are constantly trying to find out more about the potential threats posed by the industrial and agricultural **CHEMICALS** in our environment. In the past, the process was often very slow. Scientists would identify a suspected threat and study it for years, or even decades, until they felt they had proved the chemical was harmful.

Government regulators would then try to reduce or eliminate the sources of the chemical. The process could be frustrating, because the chemical had to be proved **DANGEROUS** beyond a reasonable doubt. While this slow process took place, questions and fears would continue. News reports would remind people that the research was still inconclusive and people would worry whether they were being exposed to something that could harm themselves or their children.

A boy from Masiphumelele, a slum in Cape Town, South Africa, crosses a makeshift bridge over a polluted river. Masiphumelele has just three toilets and two water taps for every 1,000 families.

# RISKY BUSINESS

Risk can be very hard to calculate. Measuring a health threat can be tricky because risk is about probabilities and trade-offs.

Some risks we choose to accept: driving a car, flying in a plane, or eating bacon cheeseburgers. Most people feel quite differently about risks they have no control over, such as chemicals in the water supply or radioactive waste—even if the mathematical risk is no higher. Risk experts will often say that we worry about the wrong things, but psychologists will say that, math aside, other factors are important.

## *Ranking Risks*

Rank these risks in order from least likely to happen to most likely to happen:

_____ **being struck by lightning**

_____ **being attacked by a shark**

_____ **being a victim of identity theft**

_____ **being hit by space debris**

_____ **a house being struck by lightning**

# CAUTION AND PRECAUTION

In recent years, many people have lobbied for a new approach to risk. Called the precautionary principle, its purpose is to guide decisions in situations where the scientific jury is still out on the safety of a new chemical or technology, but where there appears to be at least a chance of serious harm. Instead of requiring that the chemical or technology be proved to be harmful, the precautionary principle shifts responsibility to the companies to prove it is safe.

This approach follows the old sayings "better safe than sorry" and "an ounce of prevention is worth a pound of cure." The goal is to protect people—and the environment—from possible harm while scientists figure out whether there really is reason for concern.

That sounds like a good idea—at least in principle. Scientific uncertainty is unavoidable, but it shouldn't put people at risk and it shouldn't be used to postpone action that would protect people. But sometimes it might be more difficult to prove chemicals are safe than to prove they are harmful.

## PUZZLER

For risks we cannot control, whom do we trust to make the right decisions? Should decisions be made only on the basis of scientific data? What if the science is still shaky? How should other factors, such as cost, be balanced with science? In a room full of experts, whose expertise or experience should matter most?

# EPIDEMIOLOGY:
# THE BIG VIEW OF HEALTH

If the effort to understand risk is one side of the coin, the other side is epidemiology, the statistical study of health and illness in populations. There is so much in medicine that can't be proved by simple cause and effect. Or at least it can't be proved in every patient. Health experts know that smoking leads to terrible health problems, but they can't predict exactly which smokers will—or won't—have lung cancer, emphysema, or a heart attack.

Instead, researchers rely on statistical studies of entire populations. Looking at thousands of people allows them to see the subtle health effects of, say, eating nuts or exercising 30 minutes every day or gaining 20 pounds in middle age. The same result will not be seen in every person. But the overall effect can be seen, in statistically significant ways, when the researchers look at populations.

Epidemiology is the medical cornerstone of environmental justice. Nearly every aspect of public health is studied by epidemiologists. Can bed nets prevent malaria in Africa? Do measles vaccines save lives? Do vending machines in schools really contribute to obesity? Not every child living near an incinerator will develop asthma, nor will every adult living near a hazardous waste site develop cancer. It's statistics that tell the larger story. And this puts risk assessment into context. Epidemiology gives statistics life-and-death importance.

**CASE STUDY NO. 4**

# Cholera in London

In 1854, London was enduring one of its recurring epidemics of cholera, which would sweep through the city and kill thousands. Medical experts did not know what caused cholera. Sometimes healthy people became violently ill and died in less than 24 hours.

John Snow was a London physician struggling to contain a neighborhood outbreak of the disease. On a hunch, Snow decided to map the locations where the cholera victims lived. After studying the map, he came to an inspired conclusion. The map showed that one thing the victims had in common was that they all got their water from the Broad Street pump. Snow had the pump handle removed, and the cholera stopped.

Without knowing what germ caused cholera, and decades before there was any effective treatment, John Snow stopped a disease in its tracks.

as street corners, park benches, and even crack houses to watch as the medicines were swallowed. When all else failed, they detained patients in a locked hospital ward to ensure they took the medicines.

Within two years, new TB cases decreased by 15 percent. The next year, they fell by another 6 percent. That victory is an example of why Dr. Fujiwara wanted to be an epidemiologist. "I became interested in changing guidelines and policies in order to effect a bigger change," she says. "Instead of healing one person at a time, I wanted to heal a community."

## Paula Fujiwara

and other public health specialists had the odds stacked against them when they began to tackle New York City's tuberculosis (TB) problem in the early 1990s. New cases of the disease had nearly tripled in the preceding 15 years. The TB rate in one neighborhood was higher than in many developing countries. More than a half-dozen hospitals reported outbreaks of a multi-drug-resistant strain of the disease, and health-care workers were falling ill and dying from it.

Dr. Fujiwara and her team worked with hospitals to improve ventilation in waiting rooms and treatment areas. They also made sure that patients took their medication, in some cases visiting patients' homes and workplaces, as well

As director of the HIV department for the International Union Against Tuberculosis and Lung Disease, Dr. Fujiwara now works to improve TB and HIV programs in Benin, the Democratic Republic of Congo, Uganda, Zimbabwe, and Myanmar. Many clinics in these countries don't have running water or electricity. And there isn't enough medicine to battle the multi-drug-resistant TB and a newer strain called extensively drug resistant (XDR). Manufacturers don't have incentives to produce the drugs. "There are not enough cases for them to make it worth their while," says Dr. Fujiwara. "In public health, you're always weighing what is possible with the resources you have. You do the best you can."

# THE STRANGER SIDE OF STATS

The challenge in epidemiology is to unravel cause and effect. That isn't always simple or obvious. Instead, what is often found is a looser connection.

Let's say that a detailed statistical analysis of hair color and broken arms was conducted. In the study, redheads were found to break their arms at a rate 41 percent higher than blondes and 29 percent higher than brunettes. Sounds crazy? Well, there are stranger statistics than that!

But how could red hair really "cause" broken arms? Here's what a closer look at the link between the two might reveal. In our imaginary country, there is a general pattern to the distribution of hair color because of how and when the country was settled by different clans. Though all hair colors are found throughout the country, more blondes are in the rural north, more brunettes are along the mountainous southern and eastern coasts, and more redheads are in the cities to the west.

Next we find out that while the rural northerners travel mostly by horse and buggy and the coastal folks by small boat, people in the cities get around on bicycles. Knowing that, we can imagine that even though all bike riders—blonde, brunette, or redhead—fall off their bikes and break their arms at the same rate, a greater percentage of the country's redheads will end up with broken arms because there is a higher percentage of redheads who live and bike in the cities.

# WOMEN AND CHILDREN FIRST?

Epidemiological studies show that in many parts of the developing world, women and children are the first to feel the consequences of environmental problems. In the city of La Oroya, Peru, for example, nearly 99 percent of all children have dangerously high levels of lead in their blood because of pollution created by an enormous metal smelter. In Guatemala, women have 250 times more pesticide in their breast milk than is considered safe in cow's milk. Lead poisoning, untreated sewage, contaminated water, and indoor air pollution from cooking fires are among the most common risks that women and children face.

In many traditional societies, there is often a distinct division of labor within families. Women collect water for cooking, drinking, and other household uses. They also collect firewood, kindling, and leafy fodder as food for livestock, and tend crops and the family vegetable patch (80 percent of farmers in Africa are women). That means when drought strikes an area or when the land is damaged by erosion or pollution, or stripped of its vegetation, it is women who feel the impact first.

In western India, a group called SARTHI began working to promote rural development, which included deepening wells and installing hand pumps. SARTHI also launched a program to improve the efficiency of cooking stoves, which reduced the demand for firewood. After three years of drought, however, SARTHI realized that women had to become even more involved.

The goal was to get women to better understand the causes of the environmental problems that seemed to be getting worse. They learned how the destruction of the forest affected soil productivity, rainfall, and water supplies, which in turn created food, fuel, and health problems.

RAVEENDRAN/AFP/Getty Imag

They learned how many trees and shrubs it would take to meet their needs for firewood, fodder, and construction material. It takes 90 large trees, for example, to provide enough leaf fodder to feed one cow or buffalo for one year, and 50 trees for a goat or sheep.

More than

**1 billion**

people around the world rely on wood-burning stoves. According to a study in Nepal, the smoke pollution created by an indoor cooking stove is in some ways comparable to smoking **20** packs of cigarettes a day! The World Health Organization estimates that

**2 million**

people die each year because of indoor air pollution.

## NATURE BREAK

To see the power of solar cooking, try baking a batch of brownies with the heat of the sun. A simple solar cooker can be made from a pizza box and aluminum foil. Check out some hot ideas from these sources:

- solarcookers.org/basics/how.html
- solarnow.org/pizzabx.htm
- solarcooking.org/plans

# TOOLS FOR
# THE FUTURE

In the past 25 years, there have
been extraordinary achievements
in technology: the Internet, supersmart cell
phones, navigation systems for cars, computers that are faster,
more powerful, and just plain cooler than anyone could have
imagined even a few years ago.

In the years ahead, there will be an urgent need for engineers and
inventors to take even bigger leaps in technological innovation,
particularly when it comes to energy. Green technology, from fuel
cells to superthin solar panels to hydrogen-powered cars, has the
potential to free us from our dependence on fossil fuels—and
reverse global warming.

But designers and engineers also face the challenge of creating
low-tech green tools with high impact for the developing world.
That's meeting the challenge of environmental justice.

Basic needs such as food, water, sanitation, and public health often have a tough time attracting inventors.

Still, in the past 10 years some remarkable research programs have been launched to improve the lives of the world's poorest citizens. Some of the low-tech, high-impact inventions are:

❁ Inexpensive "straws" that filter out toxins and parasites from dirty drinking water that can cause more than a dozen tropical diseases.

❁ Small, efficient clay ovens that reduce the amount of fuel needed to cook as well as reduce the amount of noxious smoke that is responsible for respiratory illness.

❁ Wheeled containers and backpacks that make carrying water easier, saving hours and energy that girls can instead use to attend school.

❁ Efficient techniques that turn corn cobs and sugarcane waste into charcoal for cooking in areas that have been stripped of trees for firewood.

*Soar*

What invention might you want to create? What kind of invention would inspire you to take a stand for environmental justice? What kind of invention would get others to join you?

## Kelsey Minor

learned that 3 million people die each year from unsafe drinking water, so she decided to do something about it. Kelsey, a Girl Scout from Eugene, Oregon, was able to make a difference in the lives of thousands of people thanks to a simple device called a water pasteurization indicator, or WAPI.

Think of a WAPI as a thermometer that can measure only one temperature. Made from a three-inch piece of sealed plastic tubing, filled with soy wax at one end and weighted with a metal washer attached to a string, the device resembles a fishing bobber. The WAPI is submerged in a container of water, which is then placed in a reflective solar cooker to be heated by the sun. "The soy melts at 158 degrees Fahrenheit," explains Kelsey, so when the water reaches that temperature, "the soy wax rises to the top of the tube."

Although it was previously thought that water needed to be boiled in order to be safe to drink, researchers have discovered that heating water to 150 degrees Fahrenheit kills the microbes that commonly cause illness and disease. "This basically makes it possible for more families around the world to have clean water, and ultimately to save lives," says Kelsey.

In addition to working with Girl Scouts and adult volunteers, Kelsey mobilized members of her church and students at her high school. "I held WAPI workshops and we would come in to fill the tubes with soy wax."

To encourage others to start their own WAPI projects, Kelsey created a brochure and wrote a paper entitled "How to Make 1,000 WAPIs." The materials to make each WAPI cost only 33 cents, but Kelsey knew she would need seed funding for her project. "It definitely wouldn't have been possible without the community support," she says.

When you help someone you know, you often see the impact immediately—in the person's reaction to what you've done. That's gratifying! Helping someone halfway around the world might not offer immediate gratification. How would you get people to care about a distant issue you wanted to promote?

## Soar

It's a big world. How can you know more of it? Travel is a great way to gain new perspectives. Check out the Girl Scout *destinations* program and the world centers run by the World Association of Girl Guides and Girl Scouts. Maybe even consider a college semester abroad or a stint in the Peace Corps. Travel offers plenty of Nature Breaks, too!

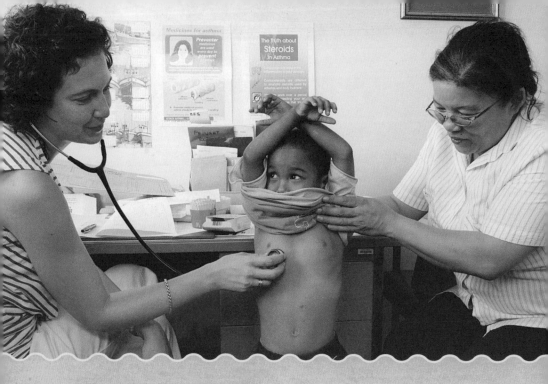

# HOT ON CAMPUS!

Global health is a hot ticket on college campuses these days. Students are filling up classrooms and lecture halls to learn about epidemics in faraway countries. At the same time, they are also getting a new perspective on some familiar chronic illnesses that plague communities much closer to home. The students come from many backgrounds and have just as many career plans, but they all share a commitment to justice.

Colleges are expanding their academic programs in public health to meet the growing demand. Many are also pioneering innovative but very practical ways to deliver lifesaving medical technologies to places in the world where they are most needed. Today, nearly 150 colleges and universities offer undergraduates the chance to earn a degree with a major or minor in public health studies. And most of these programs encourage—or require—students to do fieldwork as a part of their studies. The result is a new generation of students who are getting a firsthand look at health challenges around the world.

The boom in public health studies began in the 1990s, when the international AIDS crisis focused attention on health and justice issues around the globe. More recently, ambitious programs have been launched to stop malaria and to prevent common but deadly childhood diseases that kill millions each year. Throughout Africa, Asia, and other continents, clinics are being built and medical staff is being trained to serve poor areas, often for the first time.

The new commitment to global health involves the efforts of organizations, countries, and companies worldwide. But at the heart of this commitment are the personal decisions of individuals who want to make a real contribution. It is the pursuit and practice of justice on a global scale! Thousands of young people are volunteering around the world to participate in vaccine programs, dig wells, and build hope. The students get hands-on experience as well as a sense of how they can make a difference in their world. To help them are a growing number of programs that provide scholarships and leadership programs in public health.

The future of global health is being shaped by young people in school today. That's great news. As passionate pioneers of the high-tech revolution have said many times: "The best way to predict the future is to invent it."

## NATURE BREAK

Get together with some Ambassador friends and take a walk. Agree to walk for 15 minutes (or longer if you like!) in silence. Observe the sights and sounds of nature. Look out for signs of nature thriving despite difficult circumstances. Maybe you'll find a few stalks of grass popping up out of the snow or a tiny plant sprouting amid garbage. Ask yourself this: What does the will of nature to keep growing tell us about our search for justice?

# Continue Your Equation!

Scientific advances rely on observations, reasoning, experiments, and analysis. But sometimes the results are only estimates or probabilities, not hard facts or what can be considered scientific truth. Determine what science can—or cannot—say about an environmental threat by examining a case study you've discovered on this journey, either in this book or in articles you've collected, or something happening now in the world. What is certain about the science of the environmental threat? What issues are uncertain and why? Will more information settle the controversy? If not, why not? When does science help? When can't it?

Search out an example of a scientific finding that can be interpreted in more than one way. Ask your science teacher or visit a local community college or university, maybe even your doctor or the local office of public health. How does your source interpret the results?

Would society make different choices if we all had a better understanding of the science of environmental problems? Would there still be conflicts? When scientists disagree, whose opinions should guide the public and how?

# Deciphering Decisions

*Making decisions is hard. Reversing them is even tougher.*

But when it comes to environmental justice, reversing decisions, even decisions from long ago, is sometimes necessary.

When decisions are made, who's at the table and who isn't is always important for justice! And remember all those funny acronyms, such as NIMBY, PIITY, and LULU? Sage decision-makers move past them all and take the time to "sit at every stone." That's often the best way to get a bad decision reversed.

## CASE STUDY NO. 5
# Detroit's Big Incinerator

In February 2000, the Henry Ford Health System in Detroit announced it would shut down its medical waste incinerator after two years of community protests. The incinerator, located in a mixed business and residential community, was one of Michigan's largest. It burned 600 million pounds of waste each year.

A study had found that children living in neighborhoods surrounding the incinerator were hospitalized for asthma at rates three times higher than children from other areas of the city or county. Community activists asked how a hospital that conducts asthma research and treats asthma patients could contribute to higher asthma rates by operating an incinerator?

A dozen community, environmental, health, and citizens' groups were involved in protesting the incinerator. Demonstrations were held to educate the public and gain support, and cost-effective alternatives to incineration were presented to the hospital.

The medical center decided it could no longer live with the contradictions of being both a healer and a polluter. After hospital officials decided to close the incinerator, they consulted with the community groups and sought their help. It was a collaborative process in which the administrators treated community groups with respect and involved them in the problem-solving process.

## The Good of Greenery

Researchers in Scotland found that parks, woodland, and other green open spaces help narrow the health gap between wealthy and lower-income residents. Even small parks near low-income communities can help protect residents from strokes and heart disease, perhaps by cutting stress, boosting exercise, or both.

U.S. researchers have found that children who live in neighborhoods with more green spaces gain less weight than kids in neighborhoods with more cement and fewer trees. Having green spaces means more places for kids to play, and more exercise protects kids from obesity. But green spaces are good for the mind, too. In one study, kids with attention disorders had fewer symptoms when they read outside. And a Tokyo study found that senior citizens lived longer when they resided near green spaces. Plenty of good reasons to support green spaces and encourage people to use them!

## MORE PARKS, PLEASE

Our quality of life, and a large part of our health, involves a range of factors that include the places where we live, work, learn, and play.

Some neighborhoods have too much traffic and too much noise, too many abandoned buildings, too few parks, and too much crime. These are environmental justice issues, too. By improving the physical environment, we improve the quality of life for everyone. We also improve our national public health. *That's* justice.

# L.A.'s Cornfield

In 1959, the United Nations officially recognized a child's right to play as a fundamental human right. But for millions of children, having access to a park cannot be taken for granted. Los Angeles, the country's second largest city, has fewer acres of park per resident than any other major U.S. city. But numerous L.A. groups worked together to create Los Angeles State Historic Park in a former railyard nicknamed the "Cornfield." The 32-acre site has been a part of L.A.'s culturally and ethnically diverse history going back thousands of years to the original Native American inhabitants.

Though still under development, the park stands as a great civic accomplishment. It grew out of a shared mission and a creative solution pursued by many groups. The new park has been cheered as "a symbol of hope." Other parks have followed in other areas of Los Angeles, as well as the rest of California. They are a reminder that environmental justice is not just about correcting wrongs, but also about promoting rights.

# Erica Flores Baltodano

was always interested in local issues and local politics, "and a lot of that was fostered by my experience in Girl Scouts," she says. Baltodano brought passion and skill to her work as an intern, and later, as a lawyer, for the Center for Law in the Public Interest. The Center had just launched the ambitious project to convert L.A.'s Cornfield into recreation facilities and parks.

The goal was to bring a better quality of life and better physical health to these communities, and also to make sure the residents were involved in the planning process. "What our research demonstrated," says Baltodano, "is that different communities, different cultural and ethnic groups use parks and open space in different ways." Some appreciate solitary activities, like walking or running within a park; others are most attracted to group recreational activities and family gatherings.

"What I found fascinating," recalls Baltodano, "was that it never occurred to me how complicated it would be to create something as basic as a park for a community. What I learned was there were so many values at stake and it drew in people with so many different perspectives." Business leaders were interested because parks are good for the economic vitality of a community. The spiritual community was interested in parks as places for reflection and meditation. The public health community was interested in the health and obesity issues addressed by recreation.

"It was really a lesson in coalition building," Baltodano explains. "We were creating a common good, but approaching it from different angles depending on the values of the groups we were working with. The community learned that they can pull together and advocate and see dreams come true."

## NATURE BREAK

What do you remember best about your favorite park or playground? The swing sets or the jungle gym? The duck pond or ball fields? Or maybe it was just the grass and trees and walking around or hanging out with friends. Playgrounds and parks can be easy to take for granted. Can you imagine growing up without ever setting foot in one? Get out with some friends and be a kid again!

And while you're outdoors, scope out a true story from the animal kingdom that gives you hope for justice. How do animals look out for one another? Do you know a cat and dog who are friends? How does what you see in the animal world inform your equation for justice?

## PUZZLER

Did you ever have a friend who liked the same thing you did, but for different reasons? Maybe it was a band or a restaurant, a movie or a book, or even another friend. How did you explain it to each other? Is it really possible to value the same thing for different reasons? Is there something in your community that people value for different reasons?

## Kate Heiny

paid a lot of attention to where grocery stores were located in New Orleans when she was in college at Tulane University. It was an unusual thing for a student to notice, but it helped frame Heiny's thinking about justice.

"Nice supermarkets and high-end grocery stores would be a couple of blocks from each other, within easy access to people driving in wealthier neighborhoods," she says. "But lower-end grocery stores were a two-hour bus ride for people who lived in housing projects and didn't have a car."

How did situations like this develop, Heiny wondered, and how could they be corrected? After graduation, Heiny worked as an environmental consultant but felt frustrated. "The decisions had already been made and the problems had already occurred," she recalls. "I wanted to make an impact much earlier in that decision-making process."

Heiny also felt tugged among social, economic, and environmental issues. "One job I had was to comb through newspapers from around the world for three hours each day searching for articles that had to do with human health and environmental issues. I read so many stories about companies dumping waste and contaminating groundwater, and that made me realize that business has such a huge impact!" Heiny decided to steer her career to the source of the problem, where the opportunity to effect change was greatest.

"A decision-making process that incorporates social, economic, and environmental considerations into every decision is going to result in better, more informed decisions. And that's really the goal for me," says Heiny, who is now director of sustainability for the retail chain Target. She looks at the design and life cycles of Target's products, the company's energy efficiency and waste and water issues, its relationships with suppliers, and its impact on communities. "A holistic view of the process is what's important," she says. "The key is taking steps in the right direction and working toward better answers."

# *Add to Your Equation!*

Most decisions have to be made without perfectly complete or accurate information. This step has you taking a close look at the decision-making process to find out what works, what doesn't, and how to cope with what you don't know. If a decision affects people, chances are it affects the environment, too.

 Find an adult who has faced a difficult decision involving justice. She can be a family friend, community leader, elected official, corporate executive, or someone who works for an environmental group. The tough decision could involve building new facilities or tearing down existing ones. Ask what made the decision difficult and how she arrived at her answer. What did she know for certain and what was in doubt? Was it her decision alone or was it a group decision? Who was at the table? Who wasn't? How did she weigh different considerations and what tools did she use?

Compile a list of guidelines you could suggest for an individual or group facing a difficult decision.

When decisions are made by groups, how can you be sure they are fair? When is voting a good way to go? When is it not? Are there ways to test a decision before committing to it? How does one decision affect future decisions and what can you learn from following the "footprint" of a decision?

Owls have a reputation for being wise, but crows are smarter. They drop nuts in the road so cars will crack them open. They realized it's best to sit on electrical wires and drop the nuts in walkways. When the traffic light turns red, they safely gather the nuts.

# 6

# Create Your Equation & Present It

*The power of your equation for justice*

can be seen in the change it helps bring about, in your own life and in the lives of others. So it's time to write out your full equation and spread the word.

As you follow the presentation tips on the next pages, look for ways to share your definition of justice that will also spread your knowledge, passion, and experience. Your ultimate goal is to educate and inspire others so that they work for justice, too.

# TIPS FOR A SAGE PRESENTATION

## 1 Plan for Your Specific Audience

Now that you have your equation for justice, think about who needs to hear it. Whom could you inspire to make a big or small change in their daily lives in pursuit of justice? Would local officials think differently about whom they bring to the decision-making table if they understood the importance of "sitting at every stone"? How about your peers? What if they all Do the Math with you? What about people in your neighborhood? Is there an issue they should be aware of that needs some justice right now?

Your audience might be a mix of various people or one specific group at a small roundtable discussion with you. It's up to you! You're the Ambassador!

Tailor your presentation based on your goal for your audience. You want your definition of justice, and your equation for justice, to touch hearts and minds. That means your presentation may be a mix of visual and verbal information. Stretch yourself! Take as creative an approach as possible.

Keep in mind that being creative is not about high-tech or glossy presentations. It's about using your heart and your mind together in a fresh way.

## 2 Engage Your Audience by Giving People Something to Do!

Most people take meaning from an opportunity to immerse themselves in an experience and then think about what it means to them and how they can apply it to their lives. That's "learning by doing," and it's something you experience throughout Girl Scouting.

So, in presenting your equation for justice, can you engage small teams in a short case study? You might ask these teams to tell a story from photos and facts. Invite those in your audience to interview one another based on various questions you provide. After your audience experiences this "do," be sure to spend a little time guiding people to talk about what they realized through the activity. What did it mean to them and how will they carry its lessons forward?

## 3 Choose the Right Visuals

You've probably heard the expression "a picture's worth a thousand words." Visuals can engage us in ways that words can't. On the other hand, sometimes too many visuals can overwhelm us and we might freeze—we don't know how to act because the situation feels hopeless. So think carefully. What images will you use to describe injustice and paint the way toward justice?

# 4 Less Is Often More!

We've all been there. A boring PowerPoint presentation that drones on and on. Too much information, too much detail, or too many tangents simply invite our minds to wander!

Choose the most powerful information you have and keep it in check. It's like packing for a trip: Lay out all the clothes you think you need, then put back all the stuff that's just not necessary. Try corralling your information around the same guiding theme that you found yourself coming back to again and again as you developed your equation for justice. What's your rallying cry? Would it fit on a T-shirt or bumper sticker?

Want to be really sharp with your presentation? Observe how effective speakers organize theirs!

# 5 Be a Spark of Hope and Possibility

What will you do to inspire people to feel that change is possible and they can contribute toward it? Change doesn't have to happen all at once; a snowball effect toward justice can be a powerful start! So engage people in thinking about what they can do differently starting now, without placing any blame or feeling any guilt. If everyone does one thing (or several things!), well, Do the Math! And show the math!

# 6 Use Stories

Storytelling is a human tradition as old as the search for justice! True stories or fictional ones can move us to act on our values. What anecdotes have you gathered on your search for justice that speak to what you would like people to feel? How can you use these stories powerfully in your presentation? Think creatively. Maybe you can tell the story of people living near a waste site across the country or around the world—and then also tell the story of the people who live behind your local supermarket's Dumpster.